W9-AWQ-788

Prayers for Boys

THOMAS NELSON PUBLISHERS
Nashville • Camden • New York

Ninth printing

Copyright © 1981 by Thomas Nelson, Inc., Publishers.

Some prayers in this book are based on original material by Herbert C. Alleman, © 1966 by Thomas Nelson and Sons, Inc.

Published in Nashville, Tennessee, by Thomas Nelson, Inc. and distributed in Canada by Lawson Falle, Ltd., Cambridge, Ontario.

Printed in the United States of America.

Library of Congress Cataloging in Publication Data

Main entry under title:

Prayers for boys.

   Includes index.
   Summary: A collection of short prayers for all occasions, written especially for boys.
    1. Boys—Prayer-books and devotions—English.
[1. Prayers]
[BV283.B7A6 1981]   242'.82   81-14214
ISBN 0-8407-5241-5   AACR2

Contents

THIS BOOK
IS FOR YOU

Do you have a very special friend—a boy or a girl or a dog or a cat—that you tell everything to?

God wants you to tell your most private thoughts and feelings to Him in prayer—even the ones you think no one else will understand. This book is for that very purpose: to show you how you can talk to God freely, but respectfully, as you would talk to a good Father.

This book is for you, to keep hidden away in your drawer, or to carry with you on trips, or to put under your pillow to read at night and in the morning. Sometimes, you may even want to let your parents or your grandmother or a special friend read it with you, too. It tells you about praying, and it is divided into six sections.

I Want to Be Like You, God is an important section, for you need constantly to ask God to make you act like Him: loving, gentle, patient, self-controlled. *When I Feel . . .* is especially for those times when you need to pray but don't feel like it—like when you're angry or afraid or need forgiveness. Part III is a collection of thank you prayers—verses for mealtimes that your parents will probably remember. Part IV is for special times: your birthday, Easter, when you are sick, or before your softball game.

God wants to hear about your desires in prayer, but He also wants you to pray for other people. That's what Section V is about. Part VI, *Some Famous Prayers*, gives examples of how you might want to pray someday, too. There are prayers of Saint Augustine, John Wesley, and even Saint Patrick.

There are blank pages at the end of the book where you can write your own prayers—maybe things you want to pray for every day, or a prayer you've heard that you want to remember. There's an index on page 125 to help you when you want to go back and find one special prayer in this book.

Jesus prayed to God His Father all the time, about everything that He saw or thought or felt—and He never felt embarrassed or silly about praying. Prayer was like breathing for Him, because He knew God always wanted to listen. We hope this book will help you pray that way, too.

The Editors

Prayers for Boys

THE LORD'S PRAYER

Our Father in heaven,
Hallowed be Your name.
Your kingdom come.
Your will be done
On earth as it is in heaven.
Give us this day our daily bread.
And forgive us our debts,
As we forgive our debtors.
And do not lead us into temptation,
But deliver us from the evil one.
For Yours is the kingdom and the
    power and the glory forever.
    Amen.

MATTHEW 6:9–13

PART I

I Want to Be Like You, God

. . . The prayer of the upright is His delight.

PROVERBS 15:8

FOR A PRAYERFUL ATTITUDE

Lord, You command me to pray all the time.* Give me a prayerful attitude, so that I will talk with You as I talk with my friends. Keep me from just going through the motions and using empty words. When I do not know how to express myself, help me to be honest and sincere. Make me realize how I have neither been thankful nor sorry for my sins. Give me more love for Your Word and for Your companionship. I want to be a true disciple of You all of my life. Help me today to wait before You in prayer. In Your name, amen.

---

*1 Thessalonians 5:17

TO LOVE GOD

God, You have loved me all my life. Fill my heart with such love for You that I will be able to do the things that are pleasing to You. You are always with me and know every little thing I do, guiding and guarding me from harm. May Your goodness make me depend on You. Help me to love and serve You while this life lasts, so I will know the fullness of Your love and the sweetness of being with You in person in heaven. In Jesus Christ's name, amen.

TO LOVE OTHERS

God, You teach me in Your Holy Word that all my good works are worth nothing without love.* Put into my heart Your love, so that I can love everyone.

Help me show this love by my actions. Teach me to be loving when I watch other people. When they get into trouble, remind me how sinful I am. Show me how to help them instead of condemning them, remembering how easy it is to do wrong. Keep me from believing the worst about people. Make me quick to see when they want to do right. I want to help them by being sympathetic and a real friend. In Jesus' name, amen.

---

*1 Corinthians 13

TO BE
UNSELFISH

Lord Jesus, in Your life here You showed me the perfect example of love for others. Free me from thinking about myself all the time. You said that the one who loses life shall find it, so help me forget about putting *me* first. Teach me how to find joy in helping others, and how to give without expecting something in return. Keep the thought of Your own unselfish life always before me. In Your dear name, amen.

TO TRUST
IN GOD

God, You are powerful enough to make this world and to put me in it. Help me to trust You. My problems are small, but they are a part of Your great plan and You care about them. Make me sense Your presence with me in my daily life, and make me know that nothing can separate me from You. You watch over the birds of the air, and You tell me in Your Word that I am more valuable than the sparrows. So give me, too, the things that I need. Help me not to worry. In Jesus' name, amen.

FOR FAITH

Heavenly Father, Your Word says we are to believe and do what You say, even when doing so doesn't seem to make sense. Give me such faith. There are many things in my life which I do not understand. Help me believe that You are in control. Help me to trust You with all my heart, even when I cannot understand Your way of doing things. Show me what I need to know.

I trust You even when I do not like what is happening, knowing that You have a purpose. You make all things work together for good for those who love You.* Help me to be patient when everything seems to go wrong. Help me to walk in the footsteps of Jesus. His trust in You was perfect. By doing Your will may I learn Your truth. For Your glory.

---

*Romans 8:28

TO BE FAITHFUL

Lord Jesus, You have given each of us chores to do on earth. Teach me to be faithful as I do mine. Help me to do each one as if You were physically here with me, so that I will do the best I can. If my work is boring or harder than I thought it would be, help me to keep on and not give up, just because I am tired of it.

Teach me also to be faithful to my friends. Help me never to tell a secret. Remind me not to reveal what I overheard by accident, nor to tell things I know my friends or parents wouldn't want told. Make me worthy of trust. For Your own sake, amen.

FOR PATIENCE

Lord Jesus Christ, in Your life on earth You showed the example of perfect patience. Help me to live through my problems without complaining. Make these trials that seem so hard bring good to me. Teach me how to keep all my strength for patient waiting, and not to waste it in tears or griping.

Help me remember that all good is slow in growth, and keep me from despair because I don't see results at once. When I am aggravated with others, remind me of my own failings, and make me patient with their faults. In Your name, amen.

FOR HUMILITY

God, I know You hate the proud and give help to the humble. Make me humble. Help me to understand that the things I am proud of are gifts from You and are to be shared with others. When I am tempted to be proud and haughty, remind me that You did not give me good things because I deserved them. Teach me how to use them so they will be a blessing and not a curse to me. Lead me like a child and teach me how to trust in You. In Jesus' name, amen.

FOR
SELF-CONTROL

God, I ask You to order my mind so that I will have all my thoughts and desires under control. When temptation comes, make me ready to meet it. If fear comes over me, give me strength to conquer it. Keep me calm in danger and unruffled when panic seizes others. When I am annoyed, teach me how to talk things out kindly. If others provoke me, teach me how to settle things in love.

Give me power to control my emotions. Give me a calm that will make me able to think and work and play the best I can. Keep my trust in You unshaken. In Jesus' name, amen.

FOR STRENGTH

Lord, You know me inside out, for You made me. You know what I can do, You know what I am scared to do, and You know what I don't want to do. When my will is weak to do what I should, You be my strength. When my work is too heavy for me, lighten my load. When I am discouraged and tired, remind me that underneath me are Your everlasting arms. I want to feel Your power in my weakness. In Your name, amen.

FOR COURAGE

God, give me courage to do what I know I should do. People who put their trust in You do not need to be afraid. Help me to face this without running away. Take away any fear of being laughed at if I refuse to do what is evil. Help me stand for what is right, even if I stand alone. If I suffer pain, help me to remember Jesus, who endured the agony of the Cross without complaint. In everything I have to do, remind me that You are with me. May Your Holy Spirit comfort me. For Your glory, amen.

FOR
CHEERFULNESS

Lord, make me cheerful, so that I can make those around me glad. Remind me that the world is full of sadness and needs all the brightness I can give it. Help me give my griefs to You so that I will bring only happy thoughts to others. Help me to keep cheerfulness like a shining armor around me. When I am sad, help me not to forget that there is still joy on earth, and in a little while I will share in it again. I ask this in Jesus' name, amen.

TO BE FAIR

God, You are the Judge of all the earth. Give me the spirit of fairness. Get rid of all my mean thoughts, and make me able to see the rights of others. Keep me from being biased by the way I feel. It is so easy for me to jump to conclusions. Keep me from doing that. Help me treat others as I want them to treat me, and teach me to be fair to myself. In Jesus' name, amen.

TO BE GENEROUS

Lord, give me a generous heart, so that I am ready to give my best to others. Everything I have—time, talent, money—comes from You. I want to be willing to share it with those who need it. Make me quick to see when others do well, and to give them their just share of credit and praise.

Help me to be ready and generous with forgiveness, too. Help me to be generous to those I do not like or who seem to me not to deserve it. For Jesus Christ's sake, amen.

FOR TACT

Lord, You are full of love and mercy. Help me to be careful about other people's feelings. Keep me from saying something without thinking, or asking the wrong question—things that can hurt as badly as a slap in the face. Show me how to put shy people at ease and to give them confidence by being kind and really interested in them.

Keep me from snooping into other people's private business. Help me to be thoughtful. Bless me with keen insight so that I will see at once the right thing to do or say—or when I should be quiet. In Jesus' name, amen.

TO SAY THE
RIGHT THINGS

God, You gave me the wonderful gift of speech to share my thoughts with others. Help me to use it rightly. Teach me how to speak the truth in love, never with the wish to harm or embarrass someone else. If I know something bad about someone, help me to keep it to myself. Keep me from hateful words and from taking Your precious name in vain by using it to emphasize what I say. For Jesus' sake, amen.

FOR AN OPEN MIND

Give me, Lord, I ask, an open mind, ready to receive the truth and ready to act upon it. Show me that others have the right to their own opinions, and help me to see their point of view. Make me ready to say that sometimes I might be wrong. Help me not to shut my mind to facts simply because I do not like them. Help me to see those facts as clearly as the facts that are on my side. Open the eyes of my soul to see the truth. In Jesus' name, amen.

FOR WISDOM

God, You know that it is hard for me sometimes to know what is right. Give me the wisdom I need to see how I can please You. Thank You for Your Holy Spirit, who guides me. Help me to do what is best in Your eyes and best for those who depend on me. Give me wisdom to choose between what is false and what is true, so I will not be tricked or fooled by what looks good or my own selfishness. I ask this in Jesus' name, amen.

TO KNOW WHAT
I AM LIKE

God, You know what people are like because You made us. Teach me to know myself. Show me my weaknesses, so that I can be strong to overcome them. Keep me from being filled with pride when I should be ashamed of my own foolishness. Give me confidence in myself when there is work to be done. Help me to look at why I really want things and not to make excuses for conduct I should condemn. Make me able to see when I am wrong and to admit it. In Jesus' name, amen.

TO BE
HEALTHY

God, You have made me so wonderfully. I praise You for the body that You have given me. Help me to learn and obey all the rules that keep it healthy. Remind me of this when I eat and drink, play and work. Teach me how to love being in the fresh air, bathing in pure water, and keeping my body fit for Your service. Help me to keep a clean mind and a clean body. Make me strong so that I can do great things for You. In Jesus' name, amen.

FOR PURITY

Lord Jesus, You alone had no sin. Help me to live my life as You lived Yours. Give me a clean mind and a pure heart. Help me to turn away from the impure in word or picture. I want to keep my body as Your temple. Help me to keep out of it whatever would make it dirty.

Remind me that the pleasure of the moment is not worth the regret of eternity. Give me strength never to play around with temptation or to try to get away with as much as I can. Open my eyes so I won't try to fool myself. In Your name, amen.

FOR A
SERVANT'S HEART

Lord Jesus, You came into the world not to be served, but to serve. Give me, I pray, the heart of a servant. Help me to see what I can do for the good of others. Show me how to help those who are near me—my family, my neighbors, and my classmates at school. Make me considerate of the weak, the elderly, and the unfortunate. Show me what I can do for them. If I can help, make me glad to do it.

Teach me that a heart that looks for ways to do good for others has more happiness than the heart that does good only for *me*. By unselfish service, make me learn that it is better to give than to receive. In Jesus' name, amen.

TO LEARN
AT SCHOOL

God, You have made it a rule of life that learning is hard work. Give me an earnest heart to make the best use of my classes at school. Bless my teachers, and give me a heart to learn. Help me to continue studying hard, even when I want to quit. By doing faithfully the things I know I should, may I grow to love my work. If school work is hard for me, help me to remember that You give a crown to those who keep trying. I want to follow Jesus, who always pleased You. In His name, amen.

THE RIGHT KIND OF FRIENDS

God, help me to make the right kind of friends. Your Holy Word warns that bad company will destroy a good character.* Help me to learn how good it is not to spend time with those who do wrong or who can do nothing but make fun of other people.

Help me see that it is easier to make bad friends than it is to get rid of them. People will think that I am like the people I spend my time with. Help me to avoid the wrong kinds of friends, and instead to be a leader in doing good.

Keep me from hanging around with people who are lazy, for Satan will find mischief for idle hands to do. In Jesus' name, amen.

---

*Proverbs 13:20

TO OBEY
MY PARENTS

Lord Jesus, You were subject to Your parents. Give me, I pray, the same spirit so that, like You, I will reverently love and obey my parents. I want to love them more and more each day and to show my love by my willing obedience to what they want. Help me to obey cheerfully. Help me to be helpful. Fill me with love, so that I will honor them. In Your name, amen.

PART II

When I Feel...

. . . we do not know what we should pray for as we ought, but the Spirit Himself makes intercession for us . . .

ROMANS 8:26

WHEN I
CAN'T PRAY

God, You see that I feel like I can't pray. Fill my heart with such love for You that I will come to You in trust, knowing that You are near to help me. I don't need lots of words, for You know my most secret thoughts. I bring all my troubles and disappointments, doubts and fears to You, because You are my Father. Chase away everything that makes me doubt You. Make me know that You are always ready to hear and help me, because You love me. In Jesus' name, amen.

WHEN I'M ANGRY

God, Your Word teaches me that the fruit of the Spirit is self-control. Teach me how to be the master of myself. Give me the power to rule my own spirit. When I am aggravated or frustrated, help me to be patient. When hot words come to my lips, help me to remember that a soft answer turns away anger. Keep me calm in danger, and show me how to watch out for temptation. Help me to control my thoughts and my actions, so that You will be pleased with me. In Jesus' name, amen.

WHEN THERE'S
FIGHTING AT HOME

God, Your will is that people who live together should get along. I pray for peace in my home. You make it plain in Your Holy Word that the way to make peace is to love. Where love is, there is no fighting or quarrels. Help me to do my part in making love rule my home.

Make me thoughtful and kind. Teach me to do my tasks with a respectful and willing mind. When I want to irritate or tease my brothers and sisters, restrain me by Your love. When my feelings are hurt, remind me to turn to You for comfort so that I can still be kind. Make love rule me in everything I do and say. In Jesus' name, amen.

WHEN I
MUST DECIDE

Lord, You know how I hate decisions. Lots of people are telling me different things to do, and I am tired of listening to them. Keep me from resenting their advice, and calm me so I won't be rebellious. Lead me to do what is right. Help me not to listen to the voice of the Tempter, and to refuse the way that seems right but whose end is sin and death. In Your name, amen.

WHEN I NEED
TO FORGIVE

Lord, You tell me that if I do not forgive I will not be forgiven. Make me able to forgive others the way I want to be forgiven. Keep me from making a home for resentment in my heart. If I have wronged someone, help me to admit it. If someone has done me a wrong, help me to forgive him or her.

Clean my thoughts of all revenge, and help me to remember that trying to get even hurts me the most of all. May I forgive my friends as You forgave Your enemies. In Your name, amen.

WHEN I NEED FORGIVENESS

Lord Jesus, to whom can I go but to You with my guilty heart? You know my weakness and how I have been led into sin. You know how strong temptation can be. You were tempted in every way— but You didn't sin.

I come to You for forgiveness. You know that I love You. You know how sorry I am. Help me truly to repent, to turn away forever from the things that encouraged me to sin. If I tempted others too, show me how to help them now resist that sin. In Your name, amen.

WHEN I WANT TO LIE

God, Your eyes see all the hidden secrets of my heart. Help me to be honest, first of all with You. Make me open in all my works and deeds, and keep me from lying. May I be honest with my parents, my teachers, and my friends. Above all, keep me from encouraging others to be dishonest.

Teach me to hate lying, whether it be on my tongue or in my work. You desire truth in the very inward part of me, so take my mind and think through it. Take my heart and make it sincere. Take my lips and make them a witness for You. May I be known as a person of my word. In Jesus' name, amen.

WHEN I WANT
TO STEAL

God, I am tempted so badly to steal. Give me strength to resist. Give me such respect for the rights of others that I will not hurt them. Make me guard their belongings as I do my own. Make me honest with myself, so I will know myself for what I really am and not for what I pretend to be. Forgive me for coveting. Help me not to make it hard for others to be honest, by putting temptation in their way. I ask this in the name of Jesus Christ my Lord, amen.

WHEN I NEED MONEY

Lord, every penny on earth belongs to You. Thank You for the money You have given me. I need money for many things. Teach me how to earn it honestly. Keep me from loving money for its own sake, for the love of money is the root of evil.

If it is Your will that I should be rich some-day, show me how to use it wisely for the good of others. If it is Your will that I be poor, help me to be content, and teach me to use what I have in the best way. Help me to remember Jesus. Though he had no money, he gave all that He had—Himself—for me. In His name, amen.

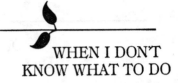

WHEN I DON'T
KNOW WHAT TO DO

God, I just don't know what to do. I can't see what is right and what is wrong. Send me light and guidance. Take my hand and lead me. Show me what You want me to do, and give me the courage and strength to do it. Guide me by Your Holy Spirit so that I won't make a mistake. I want to do what is right and best for me and those who are nearest to me. In Jesus' name, amen.

ON A GLOOMY DAY

God, my life is dark and full of sorrow. There seems to be nothing to look forward to but sadness. Show me that life still has duties and many pleasures in store for me. Revive in me the desire to live. Plant hope in my heart so that my despair will vanish, like the dew before the sun.

All good things come from You. You have promised to give them to those who love You. Fulfill Your promise to me. Give me hope in You to brighten my way here. In Jesus' name, amen.

WHEN I'M
DEPRESSED

Heavenly Father, I come to You because I need Your comfort. Nothing is going right. Everything I try to do goes wrong. I am so depressed, but I know You have a place for me and a work for me to do. Show me the place where You want me. Make me know that I can do well what You want me to do. Help me to trust in You, and to remember how much You love me. In Jesus' name, amen.

WHEN I'M TIRED
OF BEING GOOD

God, You have given me the wish to do right. Now, strengthen me to keep on doing good. When I am tired of doing right, remind me that the way of sin is hard in the end. When I am discouraged, let me feel Your presence. Help me to continue as a good disciple of Jesus Christ. In Jesus' name, amen.

WHEN I WANT
TO COMPLAIN

God, You have given me so much. I should be satisfied and happy. Keep me from the sin of ingratitude. When I complain because I do not have more, teach me to count the blessings I have. When I am unhappy because others have things I don't, make me think of what is best for me. If I am not satisfied, show me if I can change things.

Above all, keep me from griping and making others unhappy. Teach me how a merry heart has a continual feast* and makes others glad. Help me to be content with what I have, for You have said, "I will never leave you nor forsake you." In Jesus' name, amen.

---

*Proverbs 15:15

WHEN I WANT
TO WORRY

Lord Jesus Christ, You told Your disciples not to worry but to trust their heavenly Father. Help me to live without worry. Help me to trust You completely, and in quietness and in confidence to be strong.

Keep me from worrying about the past, which I cannot change, or worrying about the future, which I do not know. Help me to correct my mistakes and to put them behind me. Help me to put my hand in Yours and let Your Spirit lead me. I want Your peace, which is more than I can understand, to guard my heart and mind. In Your name, amen.

WHEN I HAVE
FORGOTTEN ABOUT GOD

God, You are my heavenly Father; yet I have forgotten You. My days have been full of what I wanted to do, without a thought of what pleases You. Open my eyes to see how this hurts You, and change my heart so that I will want to spend time with You. Help me to think of You more constantly. Teach me to pray about everything. Help me to listen for Your voice within and always to obey You. I want to devote my life to You. In Jesus' name, amen.

WHEN I SEE
SOMEONE DO WRONG

Lord, You made me my brother's keeper, but help me not to irritate my family and friends if I see them doing wrong. Teach me to say something about it once, and not to keep up a constant nagging.

Make me think of pleasant words to help them change. Encouragement will do far more than criticism. Show me when to stop talking, so that I will not make others resent me. Prevent me from making myself feel better by scolding. Help me to talk to You about it. I ask this in the name of my patient Master, Jesus, amen.

WHEN I WANT
TO TALK ABOUT OTHERS

Lord, You teach me in Your Word to love my neighbor as myself.* Keep me from hurting anyone by thoughtless words. Close my mouth, so I won't repeat stories that may not be true. Make it a rule of my life never to talk about others behind their back or to tattle. Let kindness control my tongue. Make me slow to jump to conclusions. Make me realize the words I say can never be taken back. Remind me always to think before I speak. I ask this in Your name, amen.

---

*Mark 12:31

WHEN I THINK I'M BETTER THAN ANYONE ELSE

God, You give every good and perfect gift.* Keep me from boasting about what You have given me. If I am good-looking, I should be glad. But help me to remember that my appearance did not come to me because I deserved it or worked for it. You gave it to me. Keep me from being vain.

If I am smart and do well in school, keep me from being puffed up or feeling that I am better than others whose brains work more slowly than mine. Teach me to always be aware of how small I am in this great world of yours, and how little cause I have to be conceited. In Jesus Christ's name, amen.

---

*James 1:17

WHEN I'M JEALOUS

Lord, You have given me my own special personality and all my gifts and talents. Forgive me for being jealous of those who seem to be better looking, or smarter, or richer, or more popular than I am. Teach me to work for those things I envy in them. Make me able to praise what I admire in them. Keep me from trying to tear them down by making fun or talking behind their backs. Clean my heart of jealousy, because it will only bring me unhappiness. In Jesus' name, amen.

WHEN I'M SAD

God, You are the helper of everyone who is in trouble. I come to You in my great sadness. You know how I need You. The world is dark and my heart is lonely. I am not ashamed to cry, because Jesus cried, too.

I don't ask You to take away my sorrow, for Jesus was made perfect through His suffering. But I ask You to be with me, as You were with Him. Be a father to me and comfort me as a mother comforts. Have pity on me. Make me better through this bitter experience. I ask it in Jesus' name, amen.

WHEN I'M HAPPY

God, You have filled my heart to overflowing with happiness today. Remind me to take it as coming from You.

You have filled all Your creatures with the joy of life, so that we can be glad together when we are blessed. Teach me not to be selfish when I have something to be happy about, but to share it with those who are sad or discouraged. Teach me how to enjoy being happy to the fullest, so I will have many good memories to last all my life.

I won't always be happy every day. Help me remember that today is a special gift and to take thankfully all the pleasure that is in it. In Jesus' name, amen.

PART III

Thank You, God

Oh, give thanks to the LORD, for He is good!
For His mercy endures forever.

PSALM 107:1

THANKS FOR
ANSWERED PRAYER

Lord, thank You for all Your many gifts. All good things come from You, and You have filled my life with blessings. You have given me food and clothes, a home and friends. You have given me useful chores to do and wholesome fun.

And now you have given me this special answer to prayer, satisfying the desire of my heart. What can I give back to You for all Your blessings? I can only give myself, asking You to help me enjoy my new gift in the right way. Teach me not to be selfish and to pray for others, too. Show me how to share the good things which You have given me. In Jesus' name, amen.

THANKS FOR LIFE

God, thank You for Your gift of life. You have given me a body made just right for my needs, and a mind to learn the wonders of Your world. You have made everything for me to enjoy. Help me to remember daily that I owe my life to You, and that I live in Your sight. Help me to do my best to please You while I am quick and strong. Keep me from being idle and getting into trouble. Help me to remember You, my Creator, now while I am young.* In Jesus' name, amen.

---

*Ecclesiastes 12:1

THANKS FOR HOME

Heavenly Father, I praise You for giving me a good home. When I was a helpless baby my parents cared for me. Because they loved me they gave me everything I needed. Help me to remember how they have worked for me. When I am tempted to be impatient with their rules and restrictions, help me to remember Jesus, who loved and obeyed His parents. Keep me from sulking or being ungrateful. Show me how I can help make my home a happy place, for my family and everyone who comes to visit. In Your name, amen.

Bless, O Father, thy gifts to our use and us
to thy service. For Christ's sake, amen.

BOOK OF COMMON PRAYER

Be present at our table, Lord;
Be here and everywhere adored.
Thy creatures bless, and grant that we
May feast in paradise with Thee. Amen.

JOHN WESLEY

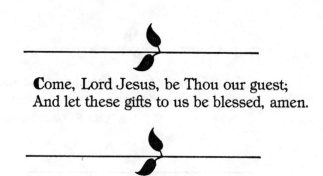

Come, Lord Jesus, be Thou our guest;
And let these gifts to us be blessed, amen.

Lord God, heavenly Father, bless us and
these thy gifts which we receive from thy bountiful
goodness. Through Jesus Christ our Lord, amen.

Bless us, O Lord, in what we are about to receive, and make us truly thankful. For Jesus Christ's sake, amen.

Give us grateful hearts, our Father, for all thy mercies, and make us mindful of the needs of others. Through Jesus Christ our Lord, amen.

BOOK OF COMMON PRAYER

Great God, Thou Giver of all good,
Accept our praise, and bless our food,
Grace, health, and strength to us afford,
Through Jesus Christ, our blessed Lord.
                                    Amen.

Thou openest Thy hand, O Lord,
The earth is filled with good;
Teach us with thankful hearts to take
From Thee our daily food. Amen.

Thou hast given so much to me,
Give one thing more—a grateful heart;
Not thankful when it pleaseth me,
As if Thy blessings had spare days,
But such a heart whose pulse may be
Thy praise.

GEORGE HERBERT

Father, we thank Thee for the night
And for the pleasant morning light
For rest and food and loving care,
And all that makes the day so fair.

Help us to do the things we should
To be to others kind and good,
In all we do, in all we say,
To grow more loving every day. Amen.

For the night's rest, the morning meal, the new day and all the blessings it may bring, we give Thee grateful thanks, our Father. Help us to serve Thee by serving our fellowman. Through Jesus Christ our Lord, amen.

PART IV

Special Times

Rejoice always; pray without ceasing; in everything give thanks; for this is the will of God in Christ Jesus for you.

1 THESSALONIANS 5:16–18

IN THE MORNING

Heavenly Father, thank You for Your care through the night and for this new day. It is a fresh page from the book of life. Help me to keep it clean and not to write anything on it that is unworthy. Protect me from evil and prevent me from doing wrong. I want to say and do only the things that please You. In Jesus' name, amen.

AT NOON

God, the sun is looking down on me like a great, all-seeing eye. Remind me now that Your eye is always on me like the sun. You are with me, not only to warn me not to sin but to assure me of Your love. May the way I live be as open as the outdoors, but may my heart be hidden with You. In Jesus' name, amen.

AT BEDTIME

Heavenly Father, thank You for this day, and thank You for being with me. Forgive me for the wrongs I have done. I want to do better tomorrow. Teach me how. Be with me as I go to bed and give me peaceful rest. Prepare me by Your gift of sleep so that I will be strong and ready when morning wakens me. Deliver me from all fear and watch over those I love. In Jesus' name, amen.

ON MY BIRTHDAY

Lord, You have given me another year of life. Teach me how to live each year as one of Your children. Your almighty protection is all around me, and I am sheltered by Your love. Keep me from evil.

Turn my thoughts to what is good, so that I will serve You with a willing mind. Help me not to forget how short and unpredictable my life is. Make me live each day so that You will be pleased with me. Give me deep thankfulness for Your love, the love of my parents, and for my many blessings. In Jesus' name, amen.

ON A TRIP

Lord, I have traveled far today, but I have not left You behind. Many miles separate me from my home and friends, but not from You. You are with me always. I praise You for Your care. Watch over me and keep me safe while I'm traveling. Open my eyes to see the beauty of Your world and the wonderful work of Your hands. Bless my family while I'm away. In Jesus' name, amen.

ON A VISIT

Heavenly Father, You have given me good friends. Watch over them and me while I visit with them. Help me to remember that I am their guest and many things are being done for my pleasure.

Remind me at all times to be grateful. Help me to show my thanks by seeing ways to help. Make me think of ways to make this visit a blessing to my friend and to myself. Remember the many boys and girls who are not so fortunate, and bring them friends who will be good to them. In Jesus' name, amen.

ON VACATION

God, please protect me on this trip and keep me in Your loving care. Make me quick to see the beauty in Your world and to appreciate it. Help me not to miss anything interesting or fun, so I will have lots of good things to remember when I get back home. There are so many things to think about, but I don't want to forget You. Show me how perfect Your handiwork is, so I can praise You better. In Jesus' name, amen.

AT CAMP

Lord Jesus, be with us and bless our camp. You took Your disciples into the mountains by themselves with no tent but the sky. You ate with them by the sea. With You they lived in the open and learned the ways of God in nature. You taught them on the hillside and walked with them through the fields.

Walk with us and talk with us in the days we spend together here. I want our camp life to be filled with Your companionship. Teach us here how to be free from worry and how to trust in You for everything we need. Keep us safe in all our outdoor sports. Thank You for those who made this camp possible. In Your name, amen.

ON A HIKE

Lord Jesus Christ, You often walked with Your disciples through the fields and by the sea. You pointed out to them the birds and the flowers, the sky and the trees. You slept under the stars and ate out in the fields.

Be with us today. Help us to see the beautiful things on earth and in the sky that are signs of our heavenly Father's love. When we are tired and hungry, make us think how You had nowhere to lay Your head, and You picked grain for food. Teach us to thank you joyfully for the world around us. Watch over us and bring us safely home. In Your name, amen.

WHEN MY PARENTS ARE AWAY

Heavenly Father, please bless and keep my parents while they are far away. Watch over them and me while we are separated. Keep them from sickness and protect them from all danger. Keep me from being lonely or afraid. Make me faithful in the things I should do. Help me to make their return happy by doing my work and bringing honor to our family name. In Jesus' name, amen.

WHEN A FRIEND DIES

Lord Jesus, You cried when Your friend Lazarus died. You know how I feel, too. Please comfort me. Help me to realize that life on earth is the beginning, not the end. Your love and mercy surround Your children here, and You go with us through death to eternal life. Thank You that if my friend knew You, he has gone to be with You, amen.

BEFORE THE GAME

God, Your Word teaches me to tell You all my requests in prayer. So I'm asking You to go with me into this game. Put my mind in order so that I will have my body under control. Keep my heart so that I will not lose my temper. Make me calm when the pressure is on. When I am provoked, give me self-control. Help me to remember that he who controls his temper is better than he who conquers a city.* Keep me within the rules of the game, and help me be honest and fair in play. For Your name's sake, amen.

---

*Proverbs 16:32

WHEN I WIN

Lord, thank You that You are with me when I win. Thank You for controlling my temper and helping me play fair. I praise You for my success. Keep me now from boasting and being overconfident the next time I play. May I remember that pride goes before destruction and a haughty spirit before a fall.* Teach me to trust in You for victory. For Your name's sake, amen.

---

*Proverbs 16:18

WHEN I LOSE

God, You comfort everyone who puts his trust in You. You know how hard it is to face failure. Help me not to be overwhelmed by my defeat. If it was my fault, help me to see my weaknesses and to do better next time. God, You can turn failure into success. Help me to learn how failure can be a blessing if it leads me to trust in You. Help me to learn that lesson now, and give me strength to try again. In Jesus' name, amen.

WHEN I'M
IN PAIN

Dear Lord, it hurts so bad I can't think of anything but the pain. Help me to bear it. Make me remember how You suffered here and how patient You were. Strengthen me so I can endure like a good child of Yours.

Heal my body, so that the pain will go away. Bless the medicine that I am taking, so it will work. Keep me from complaining all the time, from being impatient, and from just giving up. When I feel better, remind me of how good You are and how You answered my prayers. I ask these things for Your sake, amen.

WHEN I'M SICK

Lord Jesus, nothing brings me so near to You as sickness. You are the Great Doctor, and I turn to You in my weakness. I will fear nothing if You are with me.

Heal me, if it be Your will. Help me to endure this sickness patiently. Help me to remember how You never complained when You were hurting. Make me grateful for everything that is being done for me, and help me to be as little trouble as possible to those who are caring for me. Bless me and make me a blessing to those who are helping me. In Your name, amen.

IN THE HOSPITAL

Lord Jesus, thank You that You are with me now before they operate on me. You suffered for me on the Cross and You know what it is like to be afraid. Help me to be brave now, and to trust You. Give the doctor skill and wisdom. Thank You that I will be asleep while he works and won't feel any pain. Please make me well, but also teach me how I can be a comfort to others right now. In Your dear name, amen.

WHEN I'M GETTING WELL

Lord, thank You that I am feeling better. I pray now that I won't forget how You've helped me when I needed You so. I want to get well quickly. Keep me from being impatient and demanding.

Help me not to talk about how sick I've been or how awful I have felt, but to think of others. Make me considerate of my mother and father and everyone who has taken care of me for so long. Help me to be cheerful and ready to do my chores and school work again with a willing mind. In Jesus' name, amen.

ON SUNDAY

God, this is Your day, and I want to remember You first. Help me to keep the day special for You. Make me glad to go to Your house to praise You as my Lord and to hear Your good news. Above all, remind me that this is a day of joy, celebrating the resurrection of Jesus Christ from the dead. This day is Your gift to weary people; make me always grateful for it. In Jesus' name, amen.

ON THANKSGIVING

God, You have multiplied Your blessings to me and my family this year. Teach me how to be thankful with my whole heart. With my family I praise You for the land where we live and for the blessings of peace and happiness that we enjoy.

Continue to give us good rulers, and to protect us against all evil. Remind us to share our blessings with other people. Make us happy in our home today, and be with those who might be sad. In Jesus' name, amen.

ON CHRISTMAS EVE

God, You made the darkness of this night bright with the star of Bethlehem. Thank You for Jesus, Your great gift to the world. Help me to get ready for the anniversary of His birth by opening my heart to You more deeply.

Teach me to overcome my selfishness, to think more of the needs of others and less of myself. Help me to honor You in my gifts. Help me to give You the gift of a better and more unselfish life. In Jesus' name, amen.

ON NEW YEAR'S DAY

God, You just opened the door to a new year. Go with me into it. I don't know what is ahead of me, but You know. Guide me so I won't stumble, and keep me from going wrong. If I am blessed with good things, keep me humble and make me unselfish. If the darkness of sadness covers me, take my hand and make me feel how You are near. May Your Holy Spirit lead me everywhere I go. In Jesus' name, amen.

ON EASTER

Lord Jesus Christ, I rejoice in Your great victory. You have conquered death. You are risen to die never again, and those who believe and live in You will never die. Thank You that I am risen with You.

Teach me to seek the things that are above. Help me to put away what is sinful and to lead a new life. Help me to set my heart on heaven and not on the things of this world. I want to become more and more like You each day. Thank You for dying for me. In Your name, amen.

PART V

I Want to Pray for Others

I exhort first of all that supplications, prayers, intercessions, and giving of thanks be made for all men.

1 TIMOTHY 2:1

FOR MY CHURCH

Lord Jesus Christ, You have called everyone to confess You. Thank You for calling me. Thank You for putting into my heart the desire to be Your disciple. Thank You for my church, where I first confessed You as my Lord. Help me to be faithful to Your body of believers, and to love them as my spiritual family. In Jesus' name, amen.

FOR MY PASTOR

Lord, thank You for all the friends and teachers that help me to do right. I especially thank You for my pastor. Through his sympathy and interest I have learned to think more constantly of You. Bless him and keep him from all harm, and give him all the strength he needs for his work. Teach me how to listen better to Your Word as he teaches it. Show me how I can help him win other boys to You. In Your name, amen.

FOR PEOPLE WHO
ARE LONELY

Lord, You love each one of us equally. Look in tender mercy on people who feel neglected today. With You as their Friend, they will not feel alone. Make me more thoughtful of others and show me how I can bring comfort to those who are lonely. Keep me from getting too busy to notice who is lonely or sad. Teach me to be a good Samaritan and follow my love with service. In Jesus' name, amen.

FOR PEOPLE WHO
ARE NEEDY

God, Your name is Love. Hear my prayer for Your children who do not have enough to eat or wear. You have given me many good things. Open my eyes today to someone who is poor and hungry. Show me how I might help them. Show me how I can find friends for them. Lead me to other people who can help, too.

Remind me how Jesus had no place to lay His head and how He was often without food. He called the poor His brothers, and blessed those who gave to them. In His name I pray, amen.

FOR PARENTS WHO
HAVE LOST A CHILD

Heavenly Father, thank You for my life. You have taken my friend, whose parents loved him as my parents love me. Comfort them, I ask, as only You can comfort. Help them to keep their eyes on You. Remind them that You are not far away. Speak to them in their sorrow as You are speaking to me. Help them to say, "Your will be done." Show me how I can comfort them. In Jesus' name, amen.

FOR A FRIEND
WHOSE PARENT
HAS DIED

Heavenly Father, thank You for my home. Help me to remember that I did not make it, but it is Your gift to me. Give me a thankful heart for my mother and father. Remember my friend whose parent has died. Be very near to him and more to him than a father or a mother. Give me the strength to stay with him, and show me how I can comfort him.

Help us both to think of how wonderful heaven will be one day, when we are together with those we love. In Jesus' name, amen.

FOR FRIENDS AND NEIGHBORS

God, bless my friends and neighbors. Watch over their homes and shield them from all evil. Protect their houses from fire, from thieves, and anything else that might destroy or bring them trouble. Help me to be thoughtful of their property. Show me how I can serve them. Make me a ready and willing friend and good neighbor. In Jesus' name, amen.

FOR THE WORLD

Lord, You are God over this world, and You have made us all. I want Your kingdom to come in all lands. I want Your will to be done by all people. I want the light of Your gospel to shine in all the dark places of this earth. I wish people everywhere would treat each other as brother and sister. Bless those missionaries who have gone to foreign countries and keep them safe. Guide my country to send only what is good to other countries and to keep from them whatever would harm or destroy. Defeat the wicked plans that lead to war; make the peace of Christ rule the world. For His name's sake, amen.

PART VI

Some Famous Prayers

Thou art blessed, O Lord, who nourishest me from my youth, who givest food to all flesh. Fill our hearts with joy and gladness, that having always what is sufficient for us, we may abound to every good work, in Christ Jesus our Lord, through whom glory, honor, and power be to Thee forever, amen.

EARLY CHRISTIAN PRAYER

Give perfection to beginners, O Father.
Give intelligence to the little ones; give aid to those
who are running their course. Give sorrow to the neg-
ligent; give fervor of spirit to the lukewarm. Give to
the perfect a good consummation. For the sake of
Christ Jesus our Lord, amen.

IRENEUS

Look upon us, O Lord, and let all the darkness of our souls vanish before the beams of Thy brightness. Fill us with holy love, and open to us the treasures of Thy wisdom. All our desire is known to Thee. Therefore perfect what Thou hast begun and what Thy Spirit hast awakened us to ask in prayer. We seek Thy face; turn Thy face unto us and show us Thy glory. Then shall our longing be satisfied and our peace shall be perfect. Through Jesus Christ our Lord, amen.

ST. AUGUSTINE

Thanks be to Thee, my Lord Jesus Christ,
For all the benefits which Thou hast given me,
For all the pains and insults which Thou hast
   borne for me,
O most merciful Redeemer, Friend, and Brother.
May I know Thee more clearly,
Love Thee more dearly,
And follow Thee more nearly
Day by day.

ST. RICHARD

Teach us, good Lord, to serve Thee as Thou deservest; to give and not to count the cost; to fight and not to heed the wounds; to toil and not to seek for rest; to labor and not to ask for any reward, save that of knowing that we do thy will. Through Jesus Christ our Lord, amen.

IGNATIUS LOYOLA

Praise ye and bless the Lord, and give thanks unto Him, and serve Him with great humility. Amen.

ST. FRANCIS OF ASSISI

Lord, make me the instrument of Thy peace. Where there is hatred, let me sow love; where there is injury, pardon; where there is doubt, faith; where there is despair, hope; where there is darkness, light; and where there is sadness, joy.

O Divine Master, grant that I may not so much seek to be consoled as to console; to be understood as to understand; to be loved as to love: for it is in giving that we receive, it is in pardoning that we are pardoned, and it is in dying that we are born to eternal life. Amen.

ST. FRANCIS OF ASSISI

May the strength of God pilot us.
May the power of God preserve us.
May the wisdom of God instruct us.
May the hand of God protect us.
May the way of God direct us.
May the shield of God defend us.
May the host of God guard us against the
  snares of the Evil One and the tempta-
  tions of the world.

May Christ be with us.
Christ before us.
Christ over us.
May thy salvation, O Lord, be always ours
  this day
And forevermore, amen.

ST. PATRICK

In confidence of Thy goodness and great mercy, O Lord, I draw near unto Thee, as a sick person to the Healer, as one hungry and thirsty to the Fountain of life, a creature to the Creator, a desolate soul to my own tender Comforter. Behold, in Thee is all whatsoever I can or ought to desire; Thou art my Salvation and my Redemption, my Hope and my Strength. Rejoice therefore this day the soul of Thy servant; for unto Thee, O Lord, have I lifted up my soul. Amen.

THOMAS À KEMPIS

O Lord, let us not live to be useless. Amen.

JOHN WESLEY

My Own Special Prayers

*U*se these pages to write your own special prayers.

Index

INDEX

I. I WANT TO BE LIKE YOU, GOD

II. WHEN I FEEL . . .

III. THANK YOU, GOD

IV. SPECIAL TIMES

V. I WANT TO PRAY FOR OTHERS

VI. SOME FAMOUS PRAYERS

MY OWN SPECIAL PRAYERS 121